GW00632159

EDITED BY HELEN EXLEY
ILLUSTRATED BY JULIETTE CLARKE

Published simultaneously in 1999 by Exley Publications in Great
Britain, and Exley Publications LLC in the USA.

12 11 10 9 8 7 6 5 4 3 2 1

ISBN 1-86187-130-9

A copy of the CIP data is available from the British Library. All righ
reserved. No part of this publication may be reproduced in any form
Printed in China.

Exley Publications Ltd, 16 Chalk Hill, Watford, Herts WD1 4BN, UK.
Exley Publications LLC, 232 Madison Avenue, Suite 1409, NY 10016, USA

We are grateful for permission to reproduce copyright material. Whilst every
reasonable effort has been made to trace copyright holders, we would be happy
hear from any not here acknowledged. Gangaji: *For She Is T
Tree Of Life* ©1995 Valerie Kack-Brice permission of Conari Press. Frieda
McReynolds: *From A Grateful Granddaughter* permission of the author. Mavis
Nicholson: *Martha Jane And Me* published Chatto and Windus Ltd ©1991 Ma
Nicholson. Molly Parkin: *Moll: The making of Molly Parkin* ©1993 Molly Parki
published Victor Gollancz. Penny Perrick: permission of Express Newspapers. P
Smith: *Old Age Is Another Country: A Traveler's Guide* ©1995 Page Smith permis
of The Crossing Press. Lois Wyse: *Grandchildren Are So Much Fun I Should Hav
Had Them First* ©1992 Garrett Press Inc.

A LITTLE BOOK FOR MY
Grandma

A HELEN EXLEY GIFTBOOK

EXLEY
NEW YORK • WATFORD, UK

PROTECTION

Grandma's not big.
Grandma's not strong. But
when she gives me a hug the
monsters of my nightmares
slink away.

DOUGLAS MCLEAN

When I fall and cut my knees
she takes me in and laughs.
I love her gentle loving touch,
it makes me feel so safe.

KAREN WILSON, AGE 10

A PLACE FOR ME

When the household
is bristling with activity
and there seems no space
for me – I seek you out
and you shift up a bit
and find me a place beside you –
a place where I feel necessary.

JENNY DE VRIES

Brad
Ber
198?

There's a quiet place
with grandma,
where we can all find
a little peace
when our lives get too busy
and too loud.

PAM BROWN, b.1928

Grandmas can see pictures you have
painted down the telephone.

PAM BROWN, b.1928

She Understands

I recall the ocean of
unspoken love, an outpouring
deep and mysterious,
as her eyes met mine,
as if we shared complete
understanding, timeless
and ageless.

KATHLEEN MCKINNON,
FROM "QUIET WAYS"

I go round to see her every day.
She is always jolly. Every time she
laughs her tummy shakes like
jelly. She is nice and generous.
Grandma also has an apple tart in
the oven. And she has something
for me every day and there is
a lovely smell in her house.

GEMMA CURRAN, AGE 10,
FROM "TO THE WORLD'S
BEST GRANDMA"

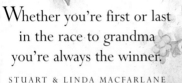

Whether you're first or last
in the race to grandma
you're always the winner.

STUART & LINDA MACFARLANE

TIME FOR YOU

A grandmother
always has time for you
when the rest of the world
is busy.

AUTHOR UNKNOWN

Grandmothers
have the time they never had
as mothers —
time to tell stories,
time to hear secrets,
time for cuddles.

DR. M. DE VRIES

THE THINGS THAT MONEY JUST CAN'T BUY

... grandparents are in a unique position to provide some of the things that money just can't buy: continuity, trust, stability, love, understanding, and unconditional support.

DR. RUTH K. WESTHEIMER
AND STEVE KAPLAN,
FROM "GRANDPARENTHOOD"

Grandmas
are good
for comfortable
snoozles and
stories.

PAM BROWN, b.1928

My grandmother
is not plump
but nice and comfortable,
when she sits you on her
knee you can nestle down
and feel safe and secure.

ANGELA DOBSON,
AGE 10
FROM "GRANDMAS
AND GRANDPAS"

Grandma's house is a treasure trove of memories; mementos fill every space and cover every wall. The wonderful smell of fresh home baking fills the air and the atmosphere exudes love and peace. Any worry, pain or sadness is quickly soothed away. Gran's house is like a giant hug.

STUART MACFARLANE

BEGINNINGS

Makes me smile to see a new
grandma — when I know
she really feels seventeen inside.

CHARLOTTE GRAY, b.1937

I thought grandmothering was part of a Serene Old Age. So what are you doing, playing goalkeeper?

. . .

Grandmothers are people who thought that life had ended — but find it beginning again.

PAM BROWN, b.1928

GRACE AND WISDOM

It is as grandmothers that our
mothers come into the fullness
of their grace.

CHRISTOPHER MORLEY (1890-1957)

Grandmothers have to have the
ability to keep their mouths shut
– till the worst blows over.
And then speak very softly.

PAM BROWN, b.1928

Grandmothers
can be more amazed,
more terrified, more delighted
than anyone else.
Their faces have got more
elastic over the years.

PAM BROWN, b.1928

I love
my grandma's wrinkles.
Every one tells a story.

TAMMY, AGE 4

... in the home
my grandmother
created, I find
the beginnings
of the love
I have inherited.

LOIS WYSE,
FROM "INHERITANCE"

LOVE AT FIRST SIGHT

A good granny
clucks over your carry-cot
the minute you're born
and says: "Well, I never did.
This is the most beautiful baby
I've ever seen in my life –
and I'm not prejudiced...."

PENNY PERRICK

Every time Grandma saw me
she said how much I'd grown,
how beautiful I was
and how clever I'd become.
Somehow just by saying it
she made it true.

BEE CHOO LIM

TWO OF A KIND

*Nature slows
grandparents to fit
exactly the pace of their
grandchildren.*

...

*The conversation between
a child and its grandmother
in the back seat of a car
always has a surreal quality.
They talk very seriously and
are inclined to burst into song.
They point at things of interest
to one another. And eventually
doze off in mid sentence.*

PAM BROWN, b.1928

ALWAYS YOUNG TO ME

I DON'T THINK
THEY WILL EVER
SEEM VERY OLD
TO ME.

PHILIP PADDON, AGED 12

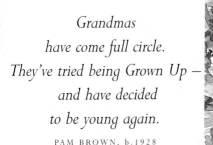

*Grandmas
have come full circle.
They've tried being Grown Up —
and have decided
to be young again.*

PAM BROWN, b.1928

GRANDMA'S THREE WISHES

If Grandma was granted three wishes:-
1) There would be world peace
2) There would be a cure for every ill
3) I would eat all my greens

HEIDI KLUM

FUN DAYS!

The ability to laugh
is the greatest gift I could receive
from my bigger-than-life
grandmother.

VALERIE
KACK-BRICE

Grandmothers
teach you interesting things —
like whistling
with two fingers
in your mouth
and making terrible faces.

PAM BROWN, b.1928

AFTER MANY YEARS
I DISCOVERED THE SECRET
INGREDIENT IN ALL
OF GRANDMA'S BAKING.
LOTS AND LOTS OF LOVE.

STUART MACFARLANE

Dearest Grandma,

Some of my friends have trendy grandmas and rich grandmas and elegant grandmas, but I like my grandma short and squashy, with her hair

on end and her glasses on
crooked and a carrier bag
full of Interesting Things.
Just like you.

NANA MNISI

BEING TOGETHER

She always says
who is this big boy and she
measures me on a bit of paper.
Then we have a cup of tea
and bread and buns.
Just the two of us.

BARRY O'CALLAGHAN

*It's so important for
a child to share something
with an older person.
A day here and there
a story shared
a laugh or cry.*

CHARLES & ANN MORSE

SPARE PARTS AND WRINKLES

If I really begged her,
Nanny would take her
teeth out and smile
at me.
I never saw anything
so funny in my life.

CAROL BURNETT

Grandmothers are
fascinating in close-up.
All those crinkles and
wrinkles and whiskers
and moles.

PAM BROWN, b.1928

THE "GRANNY FACTORY"

Everyone knows that babies are brought by the stork, but where do grans come from? A recent investigation has just uncovered information which suggests that they are created at

a special "Granny Factory" near the South Pole. They are then delivered by helicopter at the very same moment that the stork is delivering a family's first baby. Although these allegations have been denied, large containers marked "Love, Patience, Affection, Devotion and Caring" were seen....

STUART & LINDA MACFARLANE

GRANDMA KNOWS ALMOST EVERYTHING!

Even the smallest grandchild
can be very useful
to their grandmother.
Showing her just how
her electronic
gadgets work.

PAM BROWN

Grandma knows best
Grandma knows everything
Grandma did my homework
for me last night…
Well, Grandma knows <u>almost</u>
everything!

STUART MACFARLANE

YOU CAN DO NO WRONG

When your mum says, "What do you think you're playing at sitting down at the table with a mucky face," your granny murmurs, "It's only clean dirt."

When your dad takes one look at your lurex ankle socks and Afghan jerkin and says, "You're

not going out like that, are you?"
your granny says, "Well I think
she looks like a picture."
And on your wedding day, she
takes your brand-new husband
aside, puts a little wrinkled hand
on his arm and hisses in his ear,
"You're a very lucky lad.
That girl could have had her pick
you know."

PENNY PERRICK

So cosy

Grandma has got a bad leg,
so she can't walk around
without her cane.
I can sit on her lap, though,
and she tells me stories
about when she was young
and I can cuddle up with her.
It sounds weird, but I like

to snuggle into her
and smell her and rub her arm
in my face. She is so cosy.
She can't walk too well,
but she can talk. And she is
the best back-rubber
in the world.

PATTY, AGE 7

TWO NAUGHTY KIDS!

When it is very hot grandmas
take you to stand in the path
of garden sprinklers in the park.
Parents ask how could you have
possibly got so wet.
And grandmas wink at you
and say nothing.

PAM BROWN, b.1928

SHOPPING LIST

Grandmothers carry in their heads a list of grandchildren's needs. New knickers, model dinosaurs, a good French dictionary, a copy of "The Little House in The Big Woods,"

a tape of Scott Joplin, lemon
puff biscuits, bright blueberry
lipstick, a portable chess set, a
pink party dress, a mouth organ
and a penny whistle, fluffy face
flannels. What would we do
without grandmothers?

PAM BROWN, b.1928

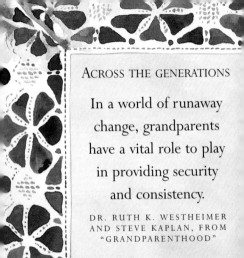

ACROSS THE GENERATIONS

In a world of runaway change, grandparents have a vital role to play in providing security and consistency.

DR. RUTH K. WESTHEIMER
AND STEVE KAPLAN, FROM
"GRANDPARENTHOOD"

Grandmothers are the archivists, the memory banks, the recorders of birthdays, anniversaries, of addresses and phone numbers, social occasions and all the things that make it possible for life to go on from day to day.

PAGE SMITH

GRANDMOTHER'S AMAZING HANDBAG

Grandmas carry: Aspirin, safety-
pins, sticking plaster, pen, pencils,
paper, crayons, small change, paper
handkerchiefs, a whistle, a spoon,
scissors, disinfectant, a comb,
lavender water, indigestion tablets,
a ping-pong ball, an eraser, a nail
file, peppermints, needle and
thread, elastic and a bus map.

PAM BROWN, b.1928

My Nana always seems to have a little tuck shop at the bottom of her bag.

FIONA WALKER, AGE 10

You're never quite sure which bulge in Grandma's bag is for you.

JOY SHIBA

GRANDMOTHERS' BONES ARE OLD.

CAROLINE CURTIS, AGE 11

My grandparents
are both about the
same age but that doesn't
seem to bother them.

ELIZABETH ROSE

Nannas always Consult Parents First.
But they bend the rules a little.

CHARLOTTE GRAY, b.1937

Grandmothers are very often
on your side – even though
they can only indicate the fact
by a clasped hand
or a surreptitious wink.

PAM BROWN, b.1928

A grandmother
will play with you, laugh with
you, talk with you, sing you songs
and tell you stories.
Just so long as you allow her
to have a little snooze
after lunch.

PAM BROWN, b.1928

One has to help grandmas
up steps. And sometimes
sit down with them, half way up.

PAMELA DUGDALE

Grandmothers
have old feet
and young hearts.

WINSTON JONES

KIND TO ME

When I am sick
you are so kind to me, you tuck
me up in the rocking chair
with my crocheted blanket and
then get me a nice, hot drink.
When I am not sick
you are just as kind to me.

HELEN HUGHES, AGE 10

SPECIAL TO YOUR LIFE

AS A GRANDMOTHER
YOU ARE SPECIAL
TO YOUR GRANDCHILD
AS NO ONE ELSE CAN BE.

DR. JOAN GOMEZ

A child who has a grandparent
has a softened view of life, the feeling
that there is more to life
than what we see, more than getting
and gaining, winning and losing.
There is a love that makes
no demands.

LOIS WYSE

COMMON GROUND

GRANDCHILDREN
AND GRANDMOTHERS
LOVE EACH OTHER
BECAUSE THEY SEE
THEMSELVES REFLECTED
IN EACH OTHER'S EYES.

STUART & LINDA MACFARLANE

*Children know
nothing:
parents know
everything.
Grandmas know
nothing too.*

PAM BROWN,
b.1928

IT IS ALL YOU

So many things we love are you!
I can't seem to explain except
by little things, but flowers and
beautiful handmade things –
small stitches. So much of reading
and thinking – so many sweet
customs.... It is all you.

ANNE MORROW LINDBERGH, b.1906

Friday was always my best day.
Not because it was the last day
of the week but because
it was the day I went to
Grandma's for lunch.
Coke and cakes.
What a treat!

And then playing cards.
I always seemed to win.
Now twenty years on, I still love
Friday lunch with gran.
The menu is the same.
Coke, cakes and cards.
And I'm suspicious that she's still
letting me win.

AMANDA BELL

I loved my granny's tiny back kitchen with its roaring fire...
I felt safe there sitting against her knees, watching her perform her domestic chores. I felt as if I never wanted to leave, that I could stay there cocooned for the rest of my life.

MOLLY PARKIN, b.1932,
FROM "MOLL;
THE MAKING OF MOLLY PARKIN"

*I accepted
her presence in my life
as if she were
a great protective tree.*

M.F.K. FISHER

A JOYOUS LOVE

She was my pillar of unconditional
love. In a childhood that was
mostly unhappy, she shines brightly
as the protective angel, the willing
bosom, the continual voice of
approval....
In her presence I experienced
limitless love; even when she was

sick or suffering some aspect of her personal tragedy, there was always love. When this love was met with the insensitivity of my adolescence, her response was more love.

Not a cloying, sticky, sentimental love, but a rambunctious, joyous, or sad, eternal love.

GANGAJI, FROM "MAMMY"

We'd settle to listen
to the "Happidrome".
While it was on we sometimes
played cards. If I won,
Gran would produce a sweet
from her pinafore pocket.
And if I lost she'd still produce
a sweet from her pocket.
"This is the life," she'd say.
"How lonely it would be

without you here." I'd feel so glad I was with her.

MAVIS NICHOLSON, FROM "MARTHA JANE AND ME"

... To teach me how to love

For as long as I can remember
you were always there
To teach me how to love others,
and how to love myself...

You were always there to listen,
to hold my hand, and to hug me.
Your joy for life and nurturing
care
Have been a major influence
in my life.
Thank you for being
my grandmother.

FRIEDA MCREYNOLDS

TAKING AWAY THE PAIN

Her voice is soft and gentle.
Comforting.
Taking the pain out of disappointment.
Consoling.
Wiping away the tears of sorrow.
Understanding.
She helps me in my search for me.

STUART MACFARLAN

GENTLE, KIND

Grandmas give you
the cherry off the top.

PAMELA DUGDALE

Grandma has a magic touch
and a gentle word that will cure
anything.

STUART & LINDA MACFARLANE